## Books by Wendy Drexler

*Notes from the Column of Memory*

*Before There Was Before*

*Buzz, Ruby, and Their City Chicks* (with Joan Kaplan)

*Western Motel*

*Drive-ins, Gas Station, the Bright Motels* (chapbook)

## Praise for Connie Saems

Connie Saems possesses the ability to enter fully into another artist's imaginative world, working in true sympatico. When her subject is swimming, she swims; what emerges on the page feels fluid, buoyant, and alive. In collaboration with poet Wendy Drexler's *Harvest of What Remains,* Saems creates visual echoes of Drexler's words that resemble neural pathways and a mind both scattering and striving to hold itself together. Her drawings throughout the text and the luminous watercolors of the cover deepen the book's emotional terrain. Together, Saems and Drexler offer a visually and lyrically immersive collaboration that renders a profoundly disorienting disease with tenderness and inventive power.

—Christine Bess Jones, author of *Limb of Water*

# Harvest of What Remains

POEMS BY WENDY DREXLER

DRAWINGS BY CONNIE SAEMS

LILY POETRY REVIEW BOOKS

*for Herb and for caregivers everywhere*

# HARVEST OF WHAT REMAINS

# Foreword

Dementia is not simply a disease of the patient, but affects also their loved ones, partners, families, friends, and their communities. As a neurologist working with families affected by dementia, I have witnessed the profound emotional toll it takes on patients and their caregivers. In this collection of poetry, the author opens a window into that experience with honesty, vulnerability, and grace. Through her words, we see the quiet strength required to care for a loved one as their memory fades, and we feel the deep love that persists despite the challenges.

These poems capture both the heartbreak and beauty of caregiving—moments of loss, of connection, and of resilience. They remind us of the power of love, even when it feels like the loved one might slip away. They remind us of St. Paul's first letter to the Corinthians, *Love is patient, love is kind . . . It bears all things, believes all things, hopes all things, endures all things. Love never fails.*

This book is a tribute to all caregivers, whose dedication often goes unrecognized. It offers comfort and understanding to anyone who has cared for someone with dementia, or anyone who has witnessed the slow unraveling of memory. It should be obligatory reading for all clinicians working with patients with dementia and their families as a loud and needed reminder of the moving humanity in the privilege of our responsibility.

It is a gift to be able to share in this journey through these poems, and I hope readers find the same solace and insight I have.

Alvaro Pascual-Leone, MD, PhD
Professor of Neurology, Harvard Medical School
Medical Director, Deanna and Sidney Wolk Center for Memory Health
Hebrew SeniorLife
Boston, MA, USA

# Contents

*And why would you expect me, or anyone, to grit my teeth and quietly carry my story? I could say there is a cost to carrying your truth but not telling it. I could say women have been doing this for decades and look where it's landed us. I could say I've gone and lost my narrative, and lost not only my understanding of the future but also my understanding of the past, and this is how I'm trying to find it.*

*—Maggie Smith*

# THE GREAT ARMS ALZHEIMER'S HAS WRAPPED US IN

To attend to you, oh great arms, I upend, distend,
and amend you; sling the warp and fling your weft;

divert, convert, and usurp you; embrace you, try
to trace you; interrogate and negate you; celebrate,

disdain, reframe you; stone you, atone for you;
sit home alone with you; gnaw clean the bone

of you; acquit you; flow merrily down the stream
with you; bite the peach and swallow the pit

of you; muffle my screams in an invisible seam
of you; yoke myself to the tallest tree of you, hug

your bark and pith; file smooth the roughest edge
of you; tame you with Sertraline, claim you,

name you, spite you, right you,
write and rewrite you—

VE|SAVI ITESHBONECAUGHT

ALZHEIN

ERSHIDESYOUREBU

TINMYTHROATRECONSTRUCTED

PHONEA

SAPPHICFRAGMENT&BERA

TMOUNTAIBU

*one*

RNCE

SURFOF RECONSTRUCTEDSAPPHICFRAG

TERYONTHE

MENT&

CARF

RADION O NBIBER SCIQE ONAINTO

&INTHEKITCHENNO

MA K EBE
L

# LOVE IS A WISHBONE CAUGHT IN MY THROAT

In our neighborhood of make-believe,
it's Friday all week except when
Saturday pretends to be Sunday.
Monday plays on the slide.
Tuesday rides the swings.
Wednesday has an alibi.

In our neighborhood at dawn, I ask
the daisies how to be brave,
how they've learned to turn
east each morning, face the sun,
follow it faithfully until dusk.
They tell me *this is our work,*
*come dark water, come frost,*
*when we will hold only the songs*
*the wind makes in the trees beside the field*
*when the birds are singing loudly.*

In our neighborhood at night,
I ask dung beetles how they roll their balls
into burrows in such straight lines,
guided only by light from the Milky Way
and snapshots of the stars
they've stored in their brains.

In our neighborhood,
Thursday hides under a hill.
Friday is out of milk.
Saturday scrambles under piles of paper.
Sunday runs the clothes through
the washing machine twice for good luck.

## RECONSTRUCTED SAPPHIC FRAGMENT 83

Black ink of plaque, tangles, spilled ink
of it, even in his not seeing what is
*[right here]* in plain view, the orange juice
carton on the refrigerator door, his keys
lying on the table, this new zone of twilight
that *[(now again)]* moves in and out
like sheaves of air carried offshore and then
turning back on us, *[for]* time is not on our side,
yet we are bride and groom to it, married
as the ocean is to the tide. Carry me, oh tide,
let me try to give thanks.

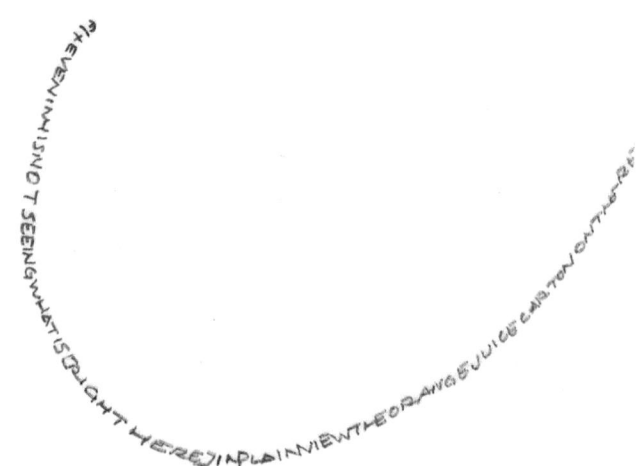

# ERASURE OF RECONSTRUCTED SAPPHIC FRAGMENT 83

     to

                  n         ight

         again

turn        s    time

                 to

           t anks.

## IN THE KITCHEN

I know what you're looking for, standing there,
holding the orange juice carton in your hand.

I ~~see~~ ∧^watch you open the cabinet that holds
coffee mugs, then turn, pondering, in the center

of the kitchen. I'm on watch here,
a watchwoman pacing the figurative

ramparts, watching and wanting to insert
a little caret of ease into the sinkhole

of your hesitation. The glasses are over there,
in the cabinet to the right of the sink, I say,

shrinking my voice to the size of a seed
so my tone will seem anecdotal, incidental,

nondirective, inflected with an orchard
of kindness. This time, my words

go down smoothly, you thank me, walk
to the right cabinet, take out a glass.

You pour your juice, and I stand there,
watching you do what you still can.

## NO WINTER

If not for the pomegranate, there would be
no winter. Save for the Buddha, no end
to suffering. Save for the carrot, there would
be no stick. Save for forgiveness, no justice.
Save for my father's secretary, my parents
might not have divorced and I in turn might
not have divorced my first husband, and I
would never have met and fallen in love
with you, and you would never have brought me
a cup of Earl Grey tea every morning
for fifteen years, nor would I have yelled
at you this morning for interrupting this poem
by pouring on the floor, for our cats, two
small piles of powdered bone broth you mistook
for cat treats. Save for the brain, no Alzheimer's.
Save for compassion, no love.

# ALZHEIMER'S HIDES YOUR CELL PHONE

Alzheimer's yells *shut up!* to two couples for talking
too loudly in a restaurant.

Insists, *I wasn't yelling.*

Doesn't realize when it is repeating itself.

Likes to make a molehill out of an ant,
and floods the lake of your last sentence.

Forgets the names of your grandchildren, hides
the months from the days, the days from the hours.

Alzheimer's packs two pairs of pajamas for the weekend
and leaves your comb and brush at home,
inserts my orthotics in your shoes, hides
your blue winter hat in my jacket,
the dirty dishes in the cupboard
the ice cream in the refrigerator,
the yogurt in the freezer.

Doesn't realize it is repeating itself.

Alzheimer's has decided it wants to spend
the rest of your life with you.

Turns the lights out one by one
but is afraid of the dark.

## AT MOUNT AUBURN CEMETERY

*Scene: The husband and wife are taking a walk
and pass another couple.*

HUSBAND: *We saw this same couple here last time.*

WIFE (blurts): *We've never–*
(internal monologue): I should stop saying we've never
seen them before. Everything is real if it's real in your mind.

For courage I'll take the panicled golden raintree that whisks
soft yellow over our heads.

I'll take the Cedar of Lebanon and the yellow-bellied
sapsucker that has drilled a ring of *rat-a-tats* around the trunk.

HUSBAND: *We see that couple every time.*

WIFE (internal monologue): The neurologist says the brain
always has to tell a story. If it can't remember the story,
it makes one up.

I'll take the heaviness of today's heat and rain, hydrangeas
spilling their milky whites onto the ground, the weeping
willow that has lost its spring-yellow sparkle.

The neurologist calls it *anosognosia*. Lack of *nosia*,
or knowledge of self, prevents accurate self-perception
of one's condition.

HUSBAND: *We see this same couple here every time.*

WIFE: *Yes, how about that? Amazing, isn't it?*

I'll take the heron drawing its neck into a flexible question mark.

7

## ON THE CAR RADIO, VON BIBER'S "CIACONA IN D MAJOR"

I begin to listen, not to the melody, but from the ground up,
                    to the bass line that repeats
               every eight bars, a trampoline
          to the trees weaving the melody
to the roots, which hold everything,
               free me, pilgrim me, loose a murmuration
                    of starlings that swirl away but always return,
                              violin and bass interlacing

with tremolos of delight, relief's glissando, syncopating
               in synchrony, each voice knowing how to give, when
          to take, exchanging codas of care. What if we could
listen to the earth the way the bass burbles up, thundering,
to the violin that roars with sunlight, turns dusky, leans in?
                    If we could hear
                         the warming ocean's shimmering dissonances?
               Become like dung beetles, navigating by the stars?

If we could listen to the water trickling over granite streambeds,
                    to the whales breaching,
*dolcissimo* and *doloroso,* at dawn, the lion padding adagio
                    over the savanna, to people in kitchens pouring
               orange juice; in alleys, humming, chanting; on subways,
reading the latest rondos of news—shootings, drought, and wildfires
                    spreading across continents?
               To the violin's squeals, dissonant, when someone's experimental

protocol has failed, or plucking pizzicato as a man on a sidewalk
               catches, in his arms, a child falling from a window,
          to the HeLa cells that keep spelling out their sorrowful sequences?
All of us curled inside the stories that run through us like vines.
                    We tangle, trying to hear each other.
               What if I could listen to you this way, darling, your voice leaning
                    against mine, mine springing lightly away from yours?

8

## HOW TO MAKE EVEN A LITTLE OF IT SLOW DOWN

At the hot pot restaurant, we dip kabocha squash, sweet as candy,
into miso broth. Lotus root dense as meat. I scald my tongue,
trying to eat too quickly. That impatience again. These days,

I can't listen to any more sad stories. Thank goodness
on the *Nature* show the endangered pangolin on the island
of Taiwan made it into the protected forest and found a mate

before the end of the breeding season. That the adorable
African bush baby, abandoned by his pregnant mother,
escaped the snake and the hostile bush babies and was able

to travel six miles in five days to the outskirts of Praetoria
where a friendly pack of bush babies welcomed him,
and suburbanites had laid out bananas on platforms linked

by ropes strung between trees. The bush babies mashed
bananas all over their happy faces and gamboled among
the ropes and trees. At the restaurant, I grab the clam

you are about to eat raw and toss it into the hot broth. I have to
watch out for you all the time now. You couldn't hear
my conversation with D and G across the table. So sweet

how you start talking to our waitress instead, teaching her
*muchas gracias* and *buenos dias,* asking her for a placemat
to write down sentences so she can talk with Latino kitchen staff

and customers. How to say *La comida está muy magnifico!
Quieres un poco de cerveza?* She tells us she's from Laos
and she squats right next to you beside our booth.

She smiles a lot. Let's say I've never seen a waitress stop to talk
to a customer for so long. Let's say we need more hope, more
bush babies who find new families and new homes.

More protected forests. More treetops and more mashing
our happy faces with kabocha squash. Let's slow it down
over a meal. Let's savor the lotus root and the bok choy

and the wrinkled cabbage leaves
we'll learn to let cool long enough
we won't burn our tongues.

## ALZHEIMER'S ABECEDARIAN

If it comes as an acrobat, you'll somersault on its teeterboard, trampoline off its walls.

If it comes as a bird, sit with it, its broken wings.

If it comes as a canteen, it will rattle *empty, empty, empty.*

If it comes as a dog, wag its tail and pat its head, use a soothing voice; try not to yell.

If it comes as an elephant, it will be the only elephant in the room.

If it comes as a faultline, tiptoe around it on eggshells.

If it comes greedily, it will take everything, leave you a pauper.

If it comes as a horse, turn its neck gently with the reins to lead it back to the barn.

If it comes as ice, remember that ice can burn even as it melts.

If it comes as a junkie, keep it from cracking its head on thunder.

If it comes as a kangaroo, you'll go everywhere in its pocket, you'll be its joey.

If it comes as laughter, it will have the last laugh.

If it comes as a mother, it will be a motherfucker.

If it comes as a nudist, you will see its bones.

If it comes as an overdose, it will overcome you with overtakelessness, that which cannot be overtaken.

If it comes as a prairie, it will take miles to cross; look for sweetgrass
to nibble along the way.

If it comes quietly, creeping in like lichen coating your branches,
it will grow so softly you won't hear it for years.

If it comes as a rifle, it will shoot bees as silently as raindrops
fall on a lake and disappear, becoming part of the lake, inseparable
from what makes a lake a lake.

If it comes as a stadium, you'll fill it with tears.

If it comes as a tiger, you are its prey—years of you to gnaw away,
licking your skin, inhaling your scent, slowly sharpening its claws.

It will come unannounced, unbridled, uncircumcised, undeniably
unearned, unforgivingly, ungraciously unhindered; uninvited, unjustly,
unkindly, and unlovingly; unmapped, unnervingly, unobtrusively-at-first,
unpacified, unquenchably unraveling; unsigned, untiringly, unurged,
unvaccinated and unwashed: un-X-rayed, unyieldingly unzipped
under everything.

It will come as vapor, at first as only mist mingling so lightly
with days of bright sun, you'll barely notice.

It will come as waves—you'll bob in its current for years, drifting
into deeper water until you too are treading just to stay afloat,
riptide trying to drag you both out. No, it comes as wind, stripping
the notes from the score, the steps from the dance, the seed
from the shell, the glue from the seal, the north from the south,
the bees from the hive, the sheets from the bed, the pink from the dawn, the
east from the west, the west from all the rest.

It comes as a Xerox copy with its own irreplaceable toner running out,
the copies getting fainter and fainter, ghostly impressions
on a nearly blank page.

It comes as yeast, rising and rising, filling the whole bowl.

It comes as a zigzag and you will breathlessly chase its shadow
across the grass, you will chase the shadow of the shadow,
the zags of the zigs and the zigs of the zags.

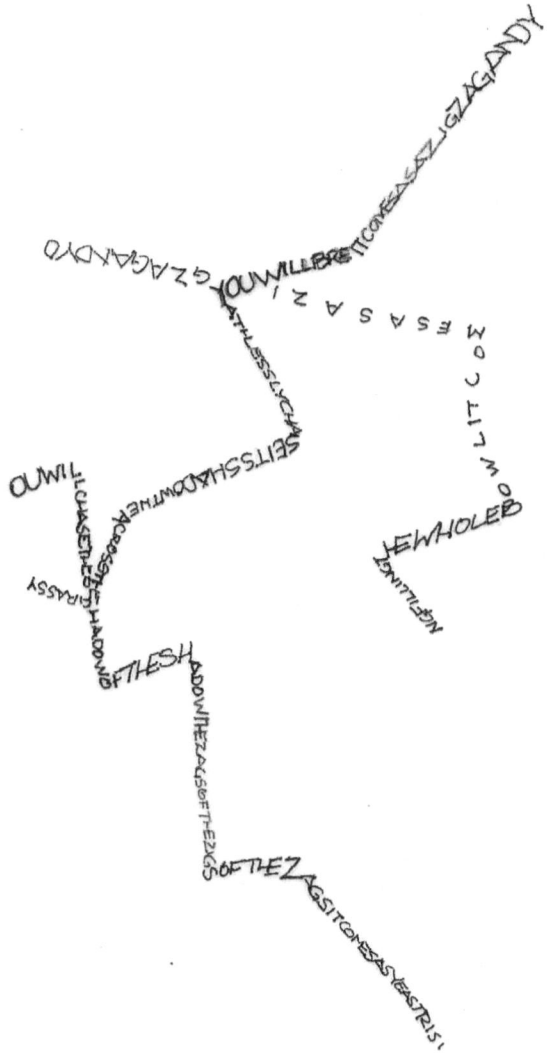

## RECONSTRUCTED SAPPHIC FRAGMENT 24C

I try to look at the big picture,

the more than twenty years we've had

together, weddings and sand dunes,

gorgeous marshes lush

with lupines and goldenrod.

Doesn't everything have its course?

The meteors, the stars mewling

and burning themselves out, and

no longer do *[we live]* as if nothing

will change. We read tea leaves

to give ourselves faith or fair warning,

as if anyone could know if what comes

of our lives will be *[the opposite]* of what

we'd once thought, foolishly *[daring]*

ourselves into trying to understand

the dark matter that has thickened

around you, like the time you said

*Next time I'll remember,* as if remembering

were a matter of will. If only we could

pour ourselves, willing and willowy,

into a vessel that can catch daylight.

## ERASURE OF RECONSTRUCTED SAPPHIC FRAGMENT 24C

the more

gorgeous

      the

  burning the

  longer

we

       try   to understand

the dark

# MARK ROTHKO, "UNTITLED," 1954

—*Yale Art Museum*

There's nothing to do but stare, nothing to do but
loosen myself in that lavender twilight in steerage
to the orange sky, which itself is drawn and quartered,
as gold as Troy, as captivating as a time-lapse video
of sunset over the Grand Canyon, as sad as a lost
address, as quenching as water for a thirst I didn't
know I had, as open as a threshold over whatever
lies beyond the body after the body. I wonder if what
the mind seeks, the body has always known but
won't tell. If the horizon is a seam too small for
transmigration, the way there's something sacred
in the hum of dust from the stained-glass windows
of Sainte Chapelle. In the rooms of "Untitled," a fire
is simmering but seemingly safe under the grate.
That kind of risk, or the relief after risk, or maybe
a truce with what, after all, can't be saved. Which is,
of course, nearly everything. But it shimmers, doesn't it,
whatever remains? Maybe it's true we are not given
more than we can bear, bounding daily from rage to

delight and back to rage I try to allay by wondering
whether to call the color of the moon outside tiger or
tarnished silver—as if I could only bridle the untitled sky
with the right shade, I'd be able to see clear through it.

OH, BRIGHT STAR

*—image from the Webb Telescope*

at the center of the Southern Ring Nebula, NGC 3132,

you are sexier than a centerfold, your dust-busting lust,

your spooling vortex, your grade-school tomfoolery,

your firebox jewelry that makes me drool,

your glossy blue stew swirling like a womb,

like a tomb, your boom-boom-boom careening roomlessly,

no midnight or noon, why, in your baby photos

you are so young, you'd just begun,

the unquiet eye of your no-end-zone

so far away from me and my home, moaning

those lonesome all-alones, no mother tongue, and, like the two of us,

star flung, dying ones, lingering and glittering and quivering

in the arc and the ache of our sun.

## JAMIE WYETH CRUSHED A STRAND OF HIS WIFE'S PEARLS,

mixed them with paint,
       tried and failed to capture
            the luminescence of a meteor
                shower. The world is better
                    because it won't last, the sun-
                        set's pink meme igniting
                            the white hulls of the boats,
                                the coast shimmering like a
                                    strand of pearls. Then *poof*—
                                        the light fades, the marina
                                            flattens—it goes so fast,
                                                the pearly light, proof that
                                                time is hungrily shredding
                                            the seconds into shadows.
                                        Hunger is Jamie Wyeth
                                        crushing a strand of his
                                        wife's pearls. Yellow-
                                            throated warblers are
                                            crushed pearls, too.
                                                Watching a bouquet of
                                                warblers swirl among
                                                leaves, fueled by hunger,
                                                I pull out of myself into
                                                their indecipherable dis-
                                                tances, rooms of branch
                                                and sky. I kneel beside a
                                                tidepool to recall how
                                                tightly barnacles hold on.
                                            Do they ever loosen?
                                        Jamie mixed the crushed
                                        pearls with white paint
                                    to stick himself to the sky.
                                    For Beauty. You can
                                die for beauty. Literally.
                            Lead white the deadliest
                        pigment. Red lake: scaled
                    beetles boiled with lye.
                Azurite from mercury
            cyanide. Yellow from ar-
        senic. Van Gogh, Correggio,
        Michelangelo—all likely
        poisoned. Take them out
    of the jewelry box, those
chokers. Wear them. Choke
on the uncrushable light.

## RECONSTRUCTED SAPPHIC FRAGMENT 145

I tell myself that caring for you isn't as hard
as lassoing the first star from the night sky,
or knowing exactly when that star was formed,
or how. I tell myself this isn't supposed to be
easy, either. I tell myself, *[do not move stones]*.
Some things take care of themselves, the way,
on any given day, you never need to count
the thousand breaths you take. Your lost
orthotics will be found. Your sore ankle will heal.
We will find the slotted metal spoon for scooping
soft-boiled eggs from the pan. Once, I made
butter just by shaking a jar filled with fresh cream,
the cream slowly thickening against the sides
of the jar. Not easy, exactly, my arm tired,
switching the jar from right to left and back.
Making butter was simple enough, a survival skill—
only the cream, a jar to hold it, and my arm, the one
the writing comes down. Some work is harder only
because you think it so. Some things take care
of themselves. That huge boulder in the pasture
doesn't need Sisyphus: the cows, untroubled, graze
around it, boulder and cows as patient as the
afternoon sun that warms the stone on cool days,
and where, on warm days, the snake finds cover.

# ERASURE OF RECONSTRUCTED SAPPHIC FRAGMENT 145

survival —

hard

trouble

and

ston

y

two

OLSTICEITSABOUTI... NEGOSSIPANDMETAPHYSICSRECONSTRUCTEDSAPPHICFRAGMENT67BERASUREOFRECONSTRUCTEDSAPPHICFRAGMENT67DOSTRANN

NINTHEPPARKINGLOT...ATTHEFUN...SHRIESTAURANT...

APPHICFRAGMENT1

ERASURE OF RECONSTRUCTED SAPPHIC FRAGMENT

## SOLSTICE

Today I'll begin again as a quiet thought
in the curl of my ear. I'll refuse to be
the snapped blade of a cheap boning knife.
The austerity is what will remain when
I give myself over to a cut lemon floating
in a glass of water, slant light streaming
through it, bubbles softly pebbling the inside
of a glass. I'll set down one more suitcase
packed with the cold provisioning each year brings,
what the body will have to give up, the hit and run
of bad hips, ligaments crowing like roosters,
the sputters and stutters of impatience.
The day cools. I've missed the sunset
but drive to the meadow anyway to watch
the failing light shuffle one second into another.
Time is a liar. It's the trees that first gather
and hold the dark. Can I learn to swagger
with the losses the way the bee, feet steeped
in pollen, staggers from blossom to blossom,
keeping on with its work?

## IT'S ABOUT TIME

I could see the sun's fast sinking, almost stone-like,
as if falling faster, speeding up, closing in on
the horizon—but the sun was moving us as steadily

as ever. You can't believe what you see, let alone
trying to fathom the void before the Big Bang.
When we were driving in Arizona last May

my iPhone flashed 9 pm and a few minutes later,
8 pm. We had entered Navaho country.
Navaho don't follow daylight saving,

knowing better than to try to mess with what
doesn't belong to the earth.

And the tediously slow hours with small children,
changing diapers, pushing the swing, the stroller,
pouring a glass of milk, another song, sleep at last!

And then the days have tumbled into years
you want back. To stand at the *still point,*
without counting, as days lap the shore

with their insistence. *Overtakelessness,*
that which cannot be gotten round (Anne Carson).

Let's say it's dark now, in the east, but there's
still some light in the west, coppery and pearly,
shawling your shoulders, awesome enough

to make you believe in the divine, or want to.
Then the navy bowl of night fills, opening to
that stillness before the stars show their faces.

I like looking up the side of a hill in October,
the tawny canopy of leaves the trees are swaddled in,
as if the hardest part were over.

It's when you're looking back you realize
the hardest part is over. Not when you're in it,
pressed like a trunk into the ground, so close

you've become what you'd feared . . .

In December woods the sky laps through
the branches after the leaves have fallen.
Maybe the trees are easier now, relieved

of their burden of holding. From where
I sit, a patch of roof across the street
burns as brightly as snow, but it isn't

snowing. Must be dew, or a slant of light—
hard to tell—and now whatever it was
has evaporated. I try to sketch the light

falling through the slats of patio chairs,
but it's the dark angularity of shadows
that holds those chairs in place.

## GOSSIP AND METAPHYSICS

I load the dishwasher, thinking about how the body belongs
to nature. How after your parents have died, you are scorched
by the stars. Of what's left, after the scattering. Noticing as well,
that we are out of Finish Jet-Dry Rinse Aide. What we want,
Akhmatova says, is gossip and metaphysics. After my stepfather's
funeral we went to see *My Big Fat Greek Wedding*. Laughed
our heads off. The jolt of being alive, the belly-splitting gift
and lift of it. Then giddy, in the mall after the movie, balancing
like a kid walking along the top of the raised wall protecting
the plantings, asking my cousins what's happened to so and so
since high school, who else has died lately. It only seems to
come to you, the gratitude, at times like that. Like that, after
the lightning strike, the cancer, the car wreck. Sometimes
I can see through the words on the page to the way the body
can hold them. Other times the words stay flat. WAKE UP!
I tell them. To help me get past what is cold and thin walled
within me. Getting closer to hurrah the way the drive-in movie
once made the world seem important, outsized. The best part
was watching the sky tint pink and purple and roll out its carpet
of stars, and the way the actors got so huge in the dark.
And how we sat on beach chairs, the tinny speakers blaring
like a chorus of frogs a quarter-croak apart, all of us a rapt
and peaceful people for the next two hours. Haven't you
lived it, too, the plague, the losses, your wrecked and ancient
childhood, each day's frantic encampments and assessments,
telling yourself in the grocery store it's OK you left your list
at home as you wonder whether loss increases love, was it
ricotta or mozzarella you needed, and the Rinse Aid
you remembered, just now.

# RECONSTRUCTED SAPPHIC FRAGMENT 67B

The bad news, your diagnosis, bombarded
my solar plexus. Now to know that neither
theory [nor] practice will alter your destination,
which is to be as inevitable as rain sliding
down a blade of grass as, unseen, [these]
your brain's cells tunnel through your corridors
like rats, snafuing [more] and ever more
neurons, rifling your range. The brain is said to be
clever, however, and born to solve problems,
to find ways to work [around] the damage,
plotting shortcuts, channeling out back roads
where [desire] still seeks passage, even
as it flies by exit signs it meant to take, unable
to see how the past has been packed into
sand castles cemented with the lacquer
of invention, that the future is a ravine.

# ERASURE OF RECONSTRUCTED SAPPHIC FRAGMENT 67B

The                          bomb



in



your brain's            rough

ver

ge



short          ing out

where

flies



invent        the future

## ODE TO THE MAN IN THE PARKING LOT
## AT THE FLYING FISH RESTAURANT

Thank you for noticing me this morning struggling
to back into the last space in the lot, partway blocked
by a poorly parked pickup truck. Thank you for that
small wave of your hand that staves off despair, turns
*can't* into *can.* Thank you for saying, when I roll
down the window, *it's tight but you can do it,* for
your *keep going,* for circling your hand for me
to turn the wheel, the way, playing jacks, I used to
circle the red rubber ball with my hand, going
around the world, scooping up the silver stars
and catching the ball before it bounced. Thank you
for raising your palm to signal *stop.* Thank you for
seeing I was in a tight place without knowing how
tight, that I'd dropped my husband off to get us
a table, and was worrying now if he would find
the hostess, if he would insult the hostess, if he
would wander down the road, if I should have
let him go in by himself, that constant watching
and worrying and wrestling and rustling into and out
of tight spaces, his mind a tight space, maybe all
it can hold are snowflakes that keep falling and
falling again and lately I'm the one with a shovel
trying to clear a path to get us a table at the Flying Fish
and a sip of that good coffee, to hear the waitress's
*What can I get you today?* and I will say, *Everything,*
while the man is over there at a table with his wife,
not noticing me, and later I realize I should have
ordered him a double latte or an espresso, I've read
people in France or Italy are doing these random acts
of kindness, though random isn't the point, I'd dropped
the ball. I'm not really blaming myself, sometimes
there are just too many sharp-pointed jacks to pick up,
the little red ball bounces and rolls away.

RECONSTRUCTED SAPPHIC FRAGMENT 19

On good days I view the way the sun riffs
on the rooftops as dazzle, on the bad days as lament,
as when I'm *[waiting]* for the light inside me to change,
or for a new scintilla of wisdom that will wash me clean,
whether through prayer, simple hope, in rituals or
*[in sacrifices]*. Sometimes I say to you *[having good]*
intentions, Sweetheart, what can I do for you today?
Yesterday, your hearing aids didn't work. I'm tired
of yelling. Someone please clean the mirror of me
so I can see my way clear, bend myself like a wood lily
to what is handsome in the everywhere, skim over
turmoil like a water strider on a pond . . .

*[but going]* on is hard *[for we know]* from the many trials
*[of works]* and deeds that the outcome is inevitable but not
the trajectory, so I tend to vacillate between the poles
of certainty and wistful thinking—how can any rock
of faith not strike hard sparks against the rasp of doubt,
especially *[after]* I saw you smothered in confusion
and you exploded, all raw impulse *[and toward]* paranoia,
as when, just yesterday, you swore at me, "You're a fucking
dictator, and you're ruining my life"!

(I must believe he *[says this]* from the part of him
that is no longer him.)

*[waiting]*      to

**bend**

**every**

**s**

**tory**    to

**raw**

**ore**

**and**   **ruin**

FIELD OF ROCKING HORSES

*—Ponyhenge, Lincoln, Massachusetts*

They are never weary, the ponies, prancing their frozen spiral
        in a field of grass—forelegs tucked beneath them, hooves
            and heads held high, their molded plastic manes

            never stained by rain, their nostrils flaring. No one knows
        who brought them here: the sawhorse, boxy body painted
with blue stars; the black stallion, rearing on hind legs;

the pink, plush-tailed filly. Riderless, bridled and brindled, tooled,
        plastic saddles rest on sturdy metal stands or wooden rockers.
            Their children who loved them, loosened from their withers.

            This is not their story. I'm not sad today, it's October, crisp,
        clear, the maples still splendid, saturated in yellow coloratura.
And because the horses circle in place, none will tire. Because

this meadow has claimed them. Because sunlight dapples their shoulders.
        Because wind and rain have come and gone and will
            come again. Because they have known the press

            of thighs and have been loved, as I have been loved.
        Because they are fresh for the morning and for all after-
noon among the bobolinks that call out to each other and the tree

swallows swooping in and out of their nest boxes and the burst cattails
        that curry the sway of their backs. Because their work is no longer
            bearing and carrying. They have been let out of the mouth

            of years—the bay, the corduroy palomino, the sorrel, the dappled,
        the dun. And because they have weathered, they are of the house
of weather and of all the homes that I have weathered. And we are not yet rust.

## AT HANSON'S FARM

I'm sitting with friends on a rusty metal folding chair
nibbling strawberry shortcake with berries we've picked
from the farm's ragged acres, biscuits we've bought from
the farm stand, vanilla ice cream we've sweet-talked
from Hanson's wife who says they sell it only on weekends
but gives it to us anyway—magic we've cobbled for the day—
when out the corner of my eye a sparrow is chasing what
looks like a smaller bird down to the ground. What's landed
isn't a bird, and what I first take for eyes are like cartoons,
a child's chalk drawing—huge black ovals as if painted on top
of the head, and below flows a two-inch long body, wing
covers speckled like rhinestones—oh, how generous
is the world to have concocted such a baroque dazzler:
an Eastern-eyed click beetle.  Praise the beetle, praise
the deception of those eyes, their beauty, told slant, eyes
as large as an owl's, flat black and the *O* of the inscribed
white eye rings. Praise the shutter of the sun's lens widening,
spring solstice just around the corner from now in the steady
click, click of the seconds. Praise my lingering here, knowing
I'll be home late for dinner, traffic will be killer,
the ice cream's melting and I'd better eat it now, better
lean into the swaggering, bountiful, buggy blue yonder,
the crumbly, slightly stale biscuits, berries with the heat
of straw still in them. Praise knowing I wouldn't want to be
like Eve, unable to savor the sweetness until after, until time
had run two-legged, out the burning gates.

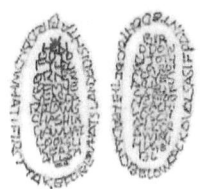

## WHETHER A FOREST IS LIKE QUICKSAND
## IF YOU'RE LOST IN IT

You won't remember the names of the wildflowers,
*coltsfoot* and *speedwell, foxglove* and *forget-me-not.*

I name them for my sake. If I can learn to listen
to the silence between your words, maybe I'll hear

meadowlarks singing the score of the hoarfrost.
Let me be nimble enough. Let there be a few

gentle hills before the heartbreak. Will there be
no end to falling? Yes, I know sagebrush

is meant to blow away. Stars die and new ones
are born. Without my consent. Nothing, I know,

will ever be as it once was. The photo of
the two of us on the wall is like light

from a distant star. When your words are gone—
oh, sing for me the trees into green.

# I ASK MY HUSBAND'S NEUROLOGIST ABOUT ALZHEIMER'S AND THE UNCANNY VALLEY

Q: Sometimes I think I love my husband more when he's clearly lost in the fog of his forest, instead of when he most resembles the person he used to be. Why?

Q: Is this like the uncanny valley, you know, the way people are attracted and responsive to a very human-looking robot until the robot looks too human and then they are repulsed?

Q: Do I have my own uncanny valley?

Q: How far must each of his synapses travel to remember where to find the tea bags in the kitchen?

Q: When I ask him how he's slept, why does he say he doesn't know yet?

Q: I first noticed his symptoms years ago, when he asked me what time we were having dinner, what time we were having dinner, what time was dinner. Why is time the first thing to go?

Q: Do the hours leave you sooner than the minutes?

Q: Where and how will this all end?

## MY HUSBAND'S NEUROLOGIST RESPONDS
## TO MY QUESTIONS ABOUT ALZHEIMER'S
## AND THE UNCANNY VALLEY

*A: When he is most like his old self, you may feel sad remembering
how dust bowl your soil is now, a candle that could blow out
with the slightest whiff. When he is fully alpine to himself,
you become most protective.*

*A: If something looks a little like us we trust it. If something looks
too much like us we are unsure if it's really human and think
someone is trying to pull a fast one. If he's lost in the fog,
that's very human. Fogs, shadows, the valley of the shadow
of death. Thou shalt not be replaced, in other words, by any robot.*

*A: I would explore the junction where your empathy locks horns
with your frustration.*

*A: Each synapse takes I-95 North to Manchester, NH, exits,
and heads south on 93 to Route 2, exit 52, formerly exit 29A,
through the rotary out Concord Avenue past the high school,
turns left at Goden Street and comes straight to your front door
into the kitchen to the cabinet to the left of the stove, bottom shelf.*

*A: Sleep is an uncanny valley and he has to check his Apnea-
Hypopnea index to know how many times he's stopped breathing.
He needs to know how many trees fell in the forest to believe
he heard any one of them fall.*

*A: Time corrals us like a barbed-wire fence, and the brain
begins to snip holes in the wires. That lets the night inside,
and the hours fly out like bats at dusk.*

*A: Minutes are a triumph of versatility. Seconds are filled with weather on all sides.*

*A: The ending can be a thousand versions of itself.*
*Loosestrife, firestorm, lichen, a leg trap, hail, a slow creek,*
*a sigh of light at the edge of a blue heath butterfly's wing.*

## I CUT MY HUSBAND'S HAIR

for the first time. Comb you through
in the kitchen, dodging covid, warily

circling like a boxer, scissor in one hand,
comb in the other. Nothing to do

but begin. That chord of fear, raking
the wet pelt forward over your eyes,

wefting a strand through the tines.
Recalcitrant, the waterfall of gray

curls up and back, and how to clamp
that strand between my two fingers

with the third hand
I need to hold the comb?

I clip imperfectly, haltingly, until my rhythm
begins to rev—*comb, straighten, lop off*—

the ragged ends along a line
of my own choosing—your locks are falling now

like confetti on your shoulders, your lap, the floor.
Lightening the weeks of our confinement.

I work my want
over your crown and down the back.

The shaver vibrates in my hand.
I sculpt the nape of your neck,

edge clean the curve of your ear

with the succinct *snip, snip* of each clip,

bending my head close, inhaling the residue
of shampoo, chamomile and coconut,

your moist scalp near and dear,
closer than I've felt all year.

# RECONSTRUCTED SAPPHIC FRAGMENT 146

It's probably better that we don't know
what will happen. Still we worry whether it'll be
as bad as we'd feared, as rosy as we'd hoped.
Don't all pomegranate seeds glisten
whether they bear fruit or only flowers?

Easy to say if there's a huge boulder in the road,
to drive around it, not try to move it. Darling,
do you remember the White Mountains in Crete,
that tree in the middle of the road we had to
drive around to get to the slow-food restaurant?
The terrifying, torturous switchbacks?

Dining at last on the terrace, overlooking
the valley, some of me was savoring
the braised lamb, purslane, the homemade bread
and cheese. Some of me was worrying about
having to return by the same road.

*[neither for me the honey nor the honeybee]*

The sweetness and the sting are inseparable.
Worry won't change that. As now, with
the boulder in the middle of our lives and how
to get around it. Offer less resistance, without
losing my habit of fierceness toward everything
I care about? Or, as Eliot says, to *sit still /*
*Even among these rocks?*

What would that sitting still look like,
and would it take my every waking hour?

Surely on this journey we won't return
by the same road.

It was raining and now the temperature
has fallen. Big wet clumps of snow hurtle
slantwise, then crisscross, then slash straight
down. Tell me, love, where do we go now?

# ERASURE OF RECONSTRUCTED SAPPHIC FRAGMENT 146

slow

terr    or

of

worrying about

losing my          everything

by the same road.

It was raining and now the temperature
has fallen. Big wet clumps of snow hurt
slantwise, then crisscross, then slash straight
down. Tell me, love, where do we go now?

## THE NIGHT BEFORE THE DAY OF ATONEMENT

*—Kol Nidre*

The strings of the cello growl, as guttural as bees,
diving through the hive of my heart, opening me
like a sidewalk split by roots—I want drums
and chants, want sharpening, want shrieks, want
to slurp the silent humming music of the spheres.
I want to bend like a wet bough, swallow my misdeeds,
cough up the bitter fruit of the year, strummed
and saved in the arms of the cello. I want to be

sealed in time's wheel of everything soon to be
revealed. I want to be carved the way Michelangelo
found David inside that rough block of marble.
I want to patch all my cracks with starlight.
Want to get lost, then found in the radius of you—
whether circle or sigh or a single leaf's drop of dew.

## WALKING THE WOODS WITH YOU
## ON THE DAY OF ATONEMENT

The rain has swelled the scent of sod's decay.
You squat to a toad, squashed except its head,
a wasp, eating its eye. So this is the way,
and wondrous, that the living are fed by the dead.
Here, sap binds the wounded flank of a maple.
Here, lichen day-glows the dark wet bark
of a fallen branch. We thread past a kettle
pond once ripped by glaciers. Mosquitoes mark

my arm. I'm their chance, as I try to greet
my fear, my damned impatience. I can't plug
each leak. We're here, your heart and mind beat
irregular time that wears us with a shrug
the way these branches must submit to air.
Next year? I hadn't meant to make a prayer.

## HARVEST OF WHAT REMAINS

Many apples ago, I climbed a crabapple tree, scrambled to pick
the round, bitter fruit. Bitter but beautiful, that hard lesson I taught
myself to keep my desire from consuming itself, like those overripe
drops that fall in the orchard, thick with bruise and blight, spreading
like split hems beneath the trees. From the harvest of what remains—
ginger golds, ambers, russets, crimsons—see how they make
a welcome mat of their dying. Then stand at the door to find out
if you will be let in or locked out, if this is to be your last supper
or splendor's summit, your squander, your reprieve, or the pulp
of sorrow. Pick yourself up from wherever you have fallen
to the ground, look around for a branch to land on, an unlatched
screen door that might open. And what will you do then with all
the light you've consumed, spellbound with mouthfuls of wonder,
when love tumbles its frantic windfall into your arms?

*three*

## NOTES FROM BAR HARBOR

Last night you yelled
*Shut up!* in a busy restaurant,
the voices like clattery rain
on an iron roof.

I covered your mouth
like a parent would
a child's / maybe

no one really noticed.

           //

I ache for the quiet of the trees
& after breakfast we walk a trail
through the woods. I try to enter

the many shades of green, wonder
how many there are. Would it
console me to name them, to create

a glossary? See them better,
as I do the trees?

*white pine  juniper  ash  oak*

Does each tree regulate its green,
pour chlorophyll to darken
variegate / brush its leaves

with acres of green?

*spruce  aspen  fern*
*celandine  verdigris  siskin*

//

This afternoon I'm reading on
the Alzheimer's Association website
that beta-amyloid plaques cluster

between nerve cells & kill
neurons. Plaques may cause
the disease or may be the byproduct—

*dis-ease* of which came first,
chicken or? & the tau protein
can turn bad & improperly fold / tangle.

You can't feel your tau folding,
no comb to tease out your tangles.

   *What day is today?*
   *How long are we staying here?*

Does tau hive / does amyloid swarm?
Does the queen ever leave for
a new colony?

     //

Why can't the neurons come
back the way the greens remember
their seasons, reassembling?

Do neurons make memories
the way you can place files
in a drawer? Do the hinges

get rusty & later you recall only
the gist & later still the gist
petrifies into drawing

a blank

*Have I had lunch yet?*
*This is 2024, right?*

//

Driving to dinner tonight
we spotted a doe and her fawn
running along the shoulder

of the highway / the fawn
bounding behind.
Were they afraid between

forest and road? Boundaries
keep what's inside from outside.
The edge of danger is where

they collide / where tau goes
bad & tangles into toxicity.

//

Rain again this morning. We visit
the Oceanarium. I won't touch
the sea stars in the touch tank

but yesterday I used my Merlin
bird app to call in the northern parula
by playing back the warbler's own song.

I know this stresses the bird
& I am inconsistent / maybe
even unethical, justify / reward

myself with a quick fix with the app
after too much hard looking
the way I yell at you after too much

hard caring. Too much trying to be /
feel normal / husband & wife
on vacation, sharing a bedroom

when we haven't shared ours
in months. Here we are in the old way
(yes & no) but now I'm all propeller,

packer, planner, finder of sunglasses,
minder of socks, night guard, meds.
This surge of untimacy / as if /

is tender & sad. As if we still were.
As if we still could. In the old ways.
This hollowing. I try to fill you

with my passions.
    *Look at that light on the water!*
You nod. Are you looking?

    *That white pine—it must have been
    sipping moonlight for 200 years!*

You've been slipping for 7 years,
maybe decades before.

*/ /*

Tonight we played Scrabble
with our friends. You couldn't
remember / wouldn't accept

that abbreviations aren't allowed.
You threw a tile across the table—
*I'm out of the game!*

Should have let you use them.
TN, DJ, CO, RN—why not?
I'd wanted to believe you were

as smart as ever. This morning
we drove to Seal Cove, clambered
out on the rocks. I love how

the smaller stones and pebbles
fill the chinks between
larger boulders. A pattern

completed like a puzzle. The way
every square inch of shore & woods
is alive—kelp, barnacles, moss, fungi,

needles, fog, bark, rain—as if
one giant inhalation / exhalation /
growth & decay so natural here

& aren't we also natural? I look up
what trees die from. Not from old age.
No senescence. More likely to die

from weather and human activities.
Your brain can't reach sunlight,
your word making is breaking down,

your memory is decomposing
& your new memories
are unable to fill in

the crevices like the rocks do.
*No abbreviations*
won't root in you.

*I'm out!* you shout.

　　　　//

Deer can't see reds & oranges,
only wave lengths of short blue
& middle green.

Deer can't see the tiger's bright
orange-and-brown-to-us stripes,
which look green to them.

This makes it harder to see
the tiger crouching in the grass.

The predators in your brain
are invisible, too.

　　　　//

Today in the woods my bones
remembered the wordlessness
of loam & bark, branch, lichen, bracken.

My hearing quickened to leaf sway,
the hard raindrops' *plop plop* bending
the rubbery leaves of the milkweed

& the leaves springing back.
In the pines, the ovenbird sang
over & over like a rock star.

It knows every inch of these woods,
every inch beholden to whatever
is living & dying. Every feather

has evolved with the quaking aspen,
the oak, the ash. With every unnamed
shade of green. The ovenbird knew

we were there, saw us seeing it *(the roses /*
*Had the look of flowers that are looked at).*
We called it in. It had no need to come.

Why should it? I think it wanted nothing of us.
You had no binoculars & no need to see it,
content in the swoon of its song. It called,

operatic, four to six *tea-chers* per second,
each *tea-cher* three to five separate notes.
Singing away in its kingdom. The notes

subsided & the silence grew thick again.
When your words are gone, I wonder
if you will remember the tunes we once sang.

*The sun will never go down,*
*go down . . . the flowers*
*are blooming forever.*

*four*

## ODE TO MY HUSBAND'S UNDERWEAR

Sunday morning and you have annoyingly
    tumbled
            onto the end of our bed
    a clean pile of your laundry.
Wanting it
out of my sight for making me stray
       from what I'd meant to do, I pull out
       your tangled undershirts, surprised by

the softened heft of the six new Lands' End Ts,
    by how tenderly
           I find I am folding the old thin Fruit
of the Looms—soon to be torn

into rags or recycled—neatly
    turning up the bottom
two thirds, tucking over the top.
        I straighten seams
       that have enveloped
your chest and belly—inhale
    Oxyclean, sun, old roses,
    clouds, and rain—
        settle them inside the drawer, then turn

to your socks, matching the Tommy Hilfigers
overstaying their years, pair their holey
soles
    and roll them
        into that sweet ball
when mate's with mate.

I praise the pilled Pumas for clinging
    to your skinny ankles, fold your briefs
into thirds the way we have

folded days into years —
  is that what makes me
want to praise the elastic bands

for cinching your waist,
  the loose leg holes that lately
gap around your thinning thighs,

the bands and seams and splices

  that holster
    your once rapid and dapper,
powerhouse of our pleasure.

## I WANT TO ASK YOU

I want to ask you if we should
waterproof the basement for $1,750.

I want to tell you when you ask
how my day was, but I know
the details will be too hard
to follow. I just say, *It was fine.*

I want you to hold and console me
when I cry over J.'s
breast cancer, but when you do,
I can't feel you feeling me.

When you ask me if I'll ever
want to make love again,
I wish I could say yes.

When you tell me you'll always
be there for me, I know you mean it,
believe it, so in that space
that hesitates between the hammer
and the anvil, I say,
*I know you will.*

I don't tell you how lonely
that makes me feel.

And here we are,
love, suspended
between the slurry
of earth and the picnic
of stars.

## LETTERS TO THE BELOVED WRITTEN ON EGG SHELLS

*—a collaboration with visual artist Connie Saems*

Grief has written letter after letter
       to her beloved, has torn them into strips,
           has seamed the broken
             words and phrases into and over
     hundreds of broken eggshells
from months of morning breakfasts,

covering the brokenness
       with the broken
            to make a residue
    of loss as unreadable
and unquenchable as Grief.

I peer into a shell, strain to read —

       OFTLY ESTERDAY NORNUMB—

           runes printed in tall thin
block letters, ghost words that ripple
       through conjecture and regret,
           the cracks between the *whys* and *what ifs.*

Grief has tossed for months on shards
       of wave-loss until the shells have become bowls
              from which Grief drinks
       from the no waters, sips
the sea change of bone-dry fragments—

       I DON'T SE LETITGO AVEN'T—

Grief has made a way-road,
       sacred carvings

along a shoreline
        where Grief might find
a place to rest among stones and sand.

        In the leaving and leavings, I search hard
                through the snipped print,
        grieving my own
beloved's WID NING FIS SURES,
        his slow DIS-
                AP PEAR ING

## TWO DEAD DOLPHINS, BLACKFISH CREEK, WELLFLEET

An acrid stench laced with ammonia,
        steeped in slow rot
                and the uncorseting of flesh.

Gutted and swollen. My son and daughter-in law,
        their baby boy, snuggled in a pack on her chest,
don't look,
        walk quickly past.

        I draw close—not sure if it's mere
fascination, to see exactly what death makes of us,

or to honor the delicate veins that mapped the flukes,
        their aerodynamic arch, their once-ease
        and power finessing the water,

and the great corsage of the intestines, spilled out,
        light brown worms swarming
        the seeping organs,

and the architecture—the gently arching nave
        of ribs that buttressed the flesh,

the orb of the now-empty eye socket,
        the long tapering snout,
                and the slightly open jaw
with its almost doll-like,
        evenly spaced rows of teeth—

and I look for a long time, consider touching,
        but do not, the forehead's
        swell of melon
            that looks as soft and vulnerable
as the fontanelles on a baby's head.

## NOTES FROM MY STRESS JOURNAL

If I'm to write what's hardest—maybe
it's what comes after I've spent eight hours

away from you with friends, a museum,
lunch, a little shopping in a store where

I stroke the stout and soft bristles and lean
wooden handles of brushes made in Germany

that can do everything—wipe up crumbs,
scrub nails and vegetables, brush your hair,

your face, sweep coffee grounds, or ashes—
then returning home, happy, exhausted, I take

a nap, wake in dusk to having to be your
everything again, the weight of what to make

for dinner, then the gift of finding forgotten
leftovers—shrimp curry in coconut milk,

only the microwave's small labor—and after,
listening with as much patience as I can as you

tell me about your day: the rain and the woman
who covered her small dog with her umbrella . . .

the woman, the umbrella, the rain, the small dog,
the small dog, the umbrella, the rain, the woman.

COUNTING MY BLESSINGS

*—for my neighbor who's lived across the street for twenty-four years*

After months of not seeing you, I almost don't
recognize you out on your driveway as one
of the several younger men who live with you

wheels you to a waiting car. How brittle, thin,
and stiff you are, like a doll, as he lifts you
from the chair, carries you to the open door,

folds you down into the seat. Once,
your MS symptoms were in remission.
Now your skin has a sheen, your insides

spinning a cocoon, consuming you. I debate
saying hello, prod myself to walk over.
Say something inane, like *Nice to see you again.*

How language fails us. *I haven't seen you
in a while, wanted to come over and say hello*
(good-bye, good-bye). *It looks like you're not*

*doing so well* (how inept!). Staring straight
ahead, you don't turn to look at me (maybe
you can't). Maybe your eyes swivel a little.

Your cheeks, hollowed out, your body as light
as the newspaper you once wrote for. This tyrant
disease, converting you to bone. But then I see

how this muscular younger man who'd carried you
in his arms to the car, after he'd settled you into
the seat, leaned over and kissed your cheek, softly,

tenderly. Whether lover or friend, caregiver, muse,
or nurse. Am I not, in a poem, supposed to tell you
I cried? And said something stupid again, there at the end,

*It looks like you're getting good care.* Did you nod?
Bob, I hope that kiss soothed your tractionless muscles,
your attenuated nerves. I hope that kiss was song.

# ANOSOGNOSIA

*One of the difficulties is that you are not aware*
*of your difficulties,* your neurologist says.
*This is not a value judgment,* he says.

*Anosognosia,* or lack of insight into your own
condition, is a fuck show, is a dog chasing its own tail.

Last week we crossed the Sonora. Feverfew. Manzanita.
Milk vetch. Rockcress. Saguaros take 75 to 100 years
to grow a first side arm. Patience is something
I lack, and your 86 billion brain cells are dry as a cactus.
At what cost do you try to hot glue them one by one?

*We are out of peanut butter.*

When you are asked what you are being treated for,
you cannot remember the word *dementia*
or the word *Alzheimer's.*

Every day I ask you not to soak the wooden spoon
in water in the sink and every day you soak it
anyway. You say we need to pick up the meds
at Walgreens we've already picked up because
the text they sent last week rides the ridge
of your mind.

There's nothing to pick up except all the pieces.
*We need to get more peanut butter.* Sometime tonight
I will find your misplaced checkbook.

Sometimes I distract you, sometimes I evade.
Is this fair? It's hard to say. We fray
and pay and pay. Relent-

less every which way.

*Must this be my subject?* John Gardner asks.

A sandstorm sweeps through your bank account.
When I check your balance the night before
your birthday, it's zero. *We are out
of peanut butter.*

## RECONSTRUCTED SAPPHIC FRAGMENT 51

Standing under that revenant umbrella
of stars last night, I realize I'm just
a rookie at this—stars as daggers,
stars as splendor?

[I don't know what to do] How long
can I keep running my life, and yours, too?
In the morning I put away the wooden
salad bowl and the spaghetti pot you've left
out on the counter, unremembering
where they go.

There seem to be [two states of mind in me],
the now, and when living as we do now
becomes impossible. I force myself
to show up to tour a memory care facility.
In the activity room, my right eye
starts twitching madly; my left is steady,
warily watching residents stay
between the thick black outlines
as they color preprinted thank-you notes
for their caregivers. Their markers,
neon yellow.

# ERASURE OF RECONSTRUCTED SAPPHIC FRAGMENT 51

Standing under

da

n

g

er,

how    to

prep

are

## ALZHEIMER'S GHAZAL

Afraid to taste the ache of losing you, I resort to distance,
fill your pill box, keep the grief at bay, court the distance.

The horizon looks hard and true but always recedes before you.
Light's diligence touches everything, imports the distance.

D. H. Lawrence says the youth and the white horse are *so silent,*
*they are in another world,* as they consort with distance.

We watch the speechless clouds braid soft knots across the sky
as we walk the pond, counting goslings to thwart our distance.

At the top of my lungs, I half sing, half scream, *O what a*
*shit-ty morning, O what a shit-ty day,* to roar at the distance.

You wake up and say, *I'm not going to my day program today.*
I tell you, *They need your help today* to restore our distance.

When you see me cry and ask me why, I shake my head, won't say.
I'd only hurt you more if I told you I've built a fort of distance.

## COGNITIVE DISSONANCE

When the young cashier at the Star Market
tells you you can't redeem four empty bottles,

you make a scene, insist she call the manager.
We're holding up the line. I tug your sleeve,

tell you again: *Each bottle is only worth 5 cents.*
But your heart is in it. You are on a crusade.

Now the manager is here: *We can't take these.*
You sharpen your insistence: *Have you changed*

*your policy?* She shakes her head. You glare.
No one dares make a move. *Let's just check out,*

I whisper, wanting this over. At home, you are
furious. *I'm never going to that market again,*

*and after we spent so much money there.*
*Almost $200. No, that was yesterday,*

*at Whole Foods*, I say. *Today was Star.* But this,
this is the dark winding stair of your mind,

this your Sisyphean task: to haul four bottles
up the mountain, and at the summit, to be

crowned with the coin of redemption.
And though the bottles are empty,

each one must weigh 50 pounds.

*

I've been listening to sound waves from
the Perseus galaxy cluster—a gazillion

accordions clenching their throats
in an endless gag. The black hole

we're being pulled toward is the one
your thoughts and memories fall into,

never to hear themselves think.
Words you no longer own.

The name for *hot pad.*
The name for *measuring spoons.*

The name of our cat.

*

In the story, Hansel left bread crumbs to mark
the trail so he and Gretel could find their way home.

When I write you a Post-it note,
*Time to leave tomorrow: 7 am,* you tear it up.

*What do you think I am, stupid?*

The scraps I leave won't help you find your way back.
And look, there are the woods. See that split oak, fallen

into the lap of another, braced there. How long
can I hold the dark in my arms? Here is the marsh.

That flash of white—great egret or snowy?
Dear one, how will I find you when you are lost

in the reeds? Let me look closer,

yellow beak or black, I'll name

that bird for you as if precision
still mattered. In the story, it's the birds

who ate the crumbs. Hungry birds,
so nothing was wasted.

## MY ANGERS

My shove-it-down-a-chute anger, give-me-a-break-or-else anger. Every
night I feed my anger a Netflix series: *The Good Wife, Law and Order
Special Victims Unit* and a bowl of popcorn sprinkled with avocado
oil, salt, nutritional yeast. My up-to-my eyeballs anger. My give-me-
the phone-and-I'll-call-a-lawyer anger. My you're-off-your-rocker
anger, god-damned what-the-hell anger. Bury my heart anger. Up-to-
its-eyeballs-in-shit anger. My escaped-convict-captured-after-three-
days-and-returned-to-her-cell anger. Frantic with worry, *you-could-
have-been-killed* anger, my *how-could you have?* Anger.

Myangersbillowintoragethattriestoswallowallmyangers.Myangers
swingbackandforthfromthechandelierthathangsfromtheceilingin
thegreatroomofangerinthegreathouseofanger.Myangersswingbackand
forthfromwalltowallandweep.

I curl fetal on the bed / want to sleep and sleep / must get up and
make dinner.

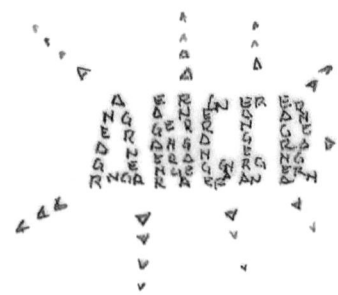

ON FINDING, IN OUR KITCHEN CUPBOARD,
THE CRACKED BATHROOM GLASS I'D THROWN IN
THE TRASH AT THE TIME-SHARE IN NEW HAMPSHIRE
*—with end words after Carl Phillip's "For Nothing Tender About It"*

I do not point out the glass to you, I'm trying not to desire
explanations, trying to keep things simple, allowing shadows
to overlap other shadows until the contours blur. Why should I
keep asking questions I know you can't answer? I should be off-

loading everything I can't expect you to explain in your endless
suspension. I shouldn't think because you're a swimmer
you should be expected to count every lap. Sure, I've known
how to find my way out of the woods, but sometimes

knowing how you once got back doesn't keep you from forgetting
the next time you're lost. Corollary: Don't tighten up.
Expect every moment to arrive at your door unarmed.

I used to get crazy when you couldn't remember a tune
we'd sung for years, or the name of a movie. Just because

I wanted you to. I tucked the glass as far down in the trash as possible.

## CLOVER FOOD LAB

He's trickling hot water meticulously over the grounds of my decaf pour-
over iced coffee, four or five passes. It's the slowness I crave. The waiting
for this coffee and I bet the black, gray, and white speckled counter is made

of an environmentally friendly non-toxic composite. I've had a hell of a day,
and while I wait I marvel at the tidy displays, bags of roasted beans,
the El Salvadorian Monte-Carlos, the Costa Rican Tarrazu, each color-coded,

printed label curated like an exhibit at MOMA. It's the order I crave.
Away from the books piled so high they sway beside my bed, the stacks
of *New York Times,* the checkbooks I've hidden from you and don't know

how to tell you, the three times today you've asked what day today is.
It's the sinuous shape of the four beakers lined up on the counter I want
with the ripe pulp of pureed juice waiting to be mixed with sparkling water.

Actually, I want everything here, I want the stainless-steel stove, the covered
cauldrons of chickpea fritters, the unblemished white tile, the minimalist,
blond good looks of the designer chairs, as if we have all day to be

at our best. I want the Pesto Breakfast Bowl with organic longwind farm
(lower case) tomatoes (why clutter up lunch with capital letters?),
a soft-boiled egg and massaged kale, I want a massaged back

and a massaged mind, for dessert I'll want the egg-free, peanut-free,
soy-free, milk-free, wheat-free Pistachio Halva. I'm going to walk out
of here scot-free and easy as a newborn babe who's played all day in Clover.

## WALKING MOUNT AUBURN CEMETERY IN THE SNOW

We walk here often so we know how to do snow
and gravestones, gravestones and snow, until

a bolt of red—a hawk plucking long thin ribbons of intestine

from the clawed-open belly of a squirrel.
Plucking and plucking the stringy integuments.

Hunger and necessity, talon and forfeit. We stop,
stare, unheeded. Dare closer, and now the hawk

half flaps, half hops away, dragging the squirrel
to higher ground. We walk on. Graves are watching

the way we pass. Sturdy, the dead. Reticence
of stones, their heft, their forecast, and the cold

so loud we have to listen, zipped tight in our parkas.
You say, *I feel so sorry for the bird* (squirrel)

*being eaten by that fox* (red-tailed hawk).
My joy is for the hawk, for his full belly, the gleam

of his yellow eye, his cold, low flapping away,
his diligence. Is this the way we balance in the world,

your empathy for the squirrel, mine for the hunger
of the hawk? I rejoice that your compassion outlasts

your remembering the words *squirrel* and *hawk,*
blurs the rhyme between *care* and *despair.*

I link my arm in yours. Our breath-clouds
nibble the air. We can last only so long

in the cold. The gravestones
are holding their hoard of snow.

*five*

# RECONSTRUCTED SAPPHIC FRAGMENT 76

It's not that the mind empties—far from it—
the mind refuses to sit still, writes agendas it
*[might accomplish]*, as it did, expertly,
once upon a time. You snap at me,
*I'm not a moron.*

*[I want to]* free you from the desert
you burn in, your mind clutching
at its calendar of lost causes—how you long
*[to hold]* on to your orphans stuck by the side
of the highway as you scan the miles of poverty
grass, feverfew, milk vetch, road killed
jackrabbits and cawing crows, saguaros
trying to grow new sidearms. In your
faded photos of the Grand Canyon,
the coyotes howl dry-eyed over ravines
of raw light. Someone
*[said]* they see better in the dark.
The coyotes. When you sit still
you can hear them breathe
down the stack of your back.

It's not that the mind empties—far from it—
the mind ill

s uck

ed
dry rav es

in the dark.
it

own s you

## REVERSING YOUR DIAGNOSIS

I steer us back to 2021 and your Camry, tomato red
as Campbell's soup—the kind my mother made with milk

to dilute the bitterness—is unsold in our driveway, and you
untake your failed driving test and unhear your neurologist

say it's unsafe for you to drive, and let's go back and I'll erase
the tangles and scrub out plaque on your PET scan so you can

boogie board with me at Good Harbor Beach
and I'll ungoosebump your skin for you

to thrill to the waves lifting you like a waiter a tray,
and now we're riding the bus in Haifa where you can unforget

the names of the tour mates you could never memorize
and lean your sweetness into me. We're moving faster now—

soon we are night dancing again in my kitchen in 2002,
the radio playing Coltrane, we have turned out the lights,

slow dancing and slow undressing, leaving our clothes
on the kitchen floor. And as we make love, we walk the shore,

Narragansett, two years before—we are just three months young
and you have given me emerald and diamond earrings

for my birthday but you won't tell me you love me—love has
slammed the door on you twice before. See how I unlatch

your heart before I take us back to the first smile I sailed
your way, a long-lost tune, somewhere between prayer and song,

igniting the air between us, plunging us past the lost surf of years
that have crested into years and the long breakers of days now

slowly sweeping you away. Please stop them here.
Hand me a buoy to keep us afloat.

## DUPLEX

My body is buoyant, displaces the air.
It's the female mosquito who needs my blood.

      The mosquito whines when it needs my blood.
      I pretend I can't hear it.

I pretend I don't have to listen to
The silence of the world that keeps falling.

      Listen to the silence that keeps falling through
      Petals of trillium, bellwort, and milkweed.

Trillium and bellwort and milkweed pedal through,
I lift a strand, snip the raveled ends.

      If I'm stranded, I snip the raveled and unruly ends
      Of the stories I tell myself to sleep at night.

Before I sleep at night, I ask myself this question:
My body, does it displace the air?

## RECONSTRUCTED SAPPHIC FRAGMENT 82B

This morning all of a sudden you asked if I'd like
some tea *[and if]* I'd slept well, in your old way,
as if *[nothing]* had changed, bringing me
my Earl Grey with almond milk in my favorite mug,
as if our intimacies had renewed, unscathed,
as if the wind were clearing a path through
our intact years, renewing us
the way the hawthorns shake off
their shelves of snow and the branches sway free.

*[but now]* I *[don't]* know how much more
will be asked of me, what I will have to give up,
culling charity or trenched with dire. I'm too much
your only. I must remember to withdraw long enough
to hear the songs the wind writes between leafless
branches—little themes gusting in unsuspecting
places, reprises of rising and falling, the patient
modulations *da capo al fine* in the key of—

Trees need winter to harden themselves
but maybe surrender is what makes
their songs *[more finely shaped]*.

# ERASURE OF RECONSTRUCTED SAPPHIC FRAGMENT 82B

**sudden**

 

 

 

 

 

 

 

**thorn**

**now**

 

 

 

 

**withdraw**

**between**

**the**    **gust**    s

 

**in**

 

 

**surrender**

# IN THIS HOLLOWING

—*with end words after Gerard Manley Hopkins's "Pied Beauty"*

Glory be that in this hollowing, some things
　Remain articulate in him, the way a cow
　　Is stamped in bone and brand, even as time swims
To stroke him light and lighter, as if winged,
　Opened, the way the earth is lifted by the plough;
　　And fits his hand in mine, smooth and trim.

Even as our days bring stress and strain most strange—
　Salad spinner in the microwave (who knows how?)
　　revealing, as I cast and reel in rooms becoming dim,
The only way to bear this ruthless change:
　　　　　Loving him.

RECONSTRUCTED SAPPHIC FRAGMENT 43

Wearing this heavy overcoat
I sometimes forget how *[beautiful he]*
of hazel eyes, of rapid wit and stubborn,
he *[stirs up still things]* best left
unstirred, unmeant, unsaid, best left
undressed *[exhaustion the mind]*.

*My* mind wants mending, rent by
how many landmarks have been erased.
Sometimes my mind *[settles down]*
when writing down the arm,
or when breathing in the cosmos.

*[but come O beloveds]*, tell me
what I have hidden from myself
*[for day is near]*.

forget *ful he*

left

mind erased.

mind *settles*

hidden from self

## HAIBUN

On our last vacation together, I ask you to wait for me on a bench out-side the bookstore. I should have known better. *Walking home,* you text, and are gone when I come out. Blessings for the 2% charge left on your cell phone. Blessings that you pick up when I call. That you can tell me the name of the street you are on. *Housatonic* from the Mohican *usi-a-di-en-uki,* "beyond the mountain place." Love, it's time for us to travel up and beyond the mountains. At the peak we must take separate paths down. When I find you brushing your teeth with a razor lathered with muscle cream, I can't tell you how terrified I am. You wouldn't under-stand. Or when you wake from a nap and try to insert your hearing aids in your mouth. We can't live together much longer in the same house. My fear may ease then, but what of sorrow deepening, what traces of sweetness will vanish? Rilke writes, *The great solitude begins,* but mine began years before, Alzheimer's whittling you like a piece of wood. My right eye twitches as I carefully fold your shirts away, into the suitcase for the trip home, clean your CPAP mask, snug it back into the padded compartment, zip up the case.

In winter's cold wind, / a window left wide open. / The future chills me.

## THE WAY THESE OPALESCENT BALLS GLOW

*—after "Pivot Points" by Rebecca Long,* Art on the Trails, *Southborough, MA*

as also the way the gravitational pull of the sun holds the planets
in the solar system in tension and suspension
in the vastness of the universe,
as even Pluto, six billion kilometers
away from us, is also so held. As even, these months
when you seem that far away, love,
suspended in an elsewhere
in the dark scatter of your mind.
I will keep trying to find
a way.

## TOWARD THE PINNACLE OF YOUR LEAVING

You don't know you're leaving, but you're
no longer safe at home. And so Rilke's

*steeply sloping hour* rises toward the pinnacle
of your leaving. I try to imagine how

it will be for you—as if you were a bird,
dropped wingless into a forest, a bird

that can't fly, can't roost, and the trees will
merge into beige wallpaper as you find

yourself among memory-care strangers,
walk past a fake fireplace, a large-screen TV,

led to a strange bed in a strange bedroom.
And how will it be for me, when I am freed

from the hundred kingdoms I keep track of?
In one, I unload my heart like a dishwasher,

plate by plate. When all the dishes are mine
alone to neatly stack and put away, I wonder

who will be bewildered, who pastured, who claimed,
who will be remaindered, who the remains.

Last night before bed, you asked, *When are we
heading out? What do you mean?* I replied,

*We're here.* I held back from saying *We're here,
home.* Because this isn't going to be your home

much longer. As if my not saying *home* would
lessen the loss. Because if I said it, the breathiness

of the soft *h* from the back of my throat,
followed by the long *om,* like a chant

from the cushion of night, would have turned
to stone in my throat.

## SITTING WITH MY HUSBAND ON A BENCH
## IN FRONT OF CLAY POND

a not-so-beautiful pond, but I like the way the leaves
form an arch over the water, the sun slanting through,
making them glow, and on the far side of the pond
we see a swan my husband refers to as "a white fish,"
which makes me think more about the solitary swan
we'd passed earlier who was sitting on the bank—
the way she was grooming herself so conscientiously—
this is her work, after all—corkscrewing her limber
and endless neck under her, nipping one feather,
then another, and then I began to listen to some water
sounds on my meditation app as I looked at the moiré
patterns the wind was making on the actual water,
and the wind was just the wind, but cool on the edges
with a slightly warm core from the warm day, and yes,
the earth is probably dying, and on the radio today
I heard the Colorado River is running out of water
and can maybe be saved if people would only eat
one less hamburger each week, which shouldn't be
a big deal but is, and I don't eat hamburger anymore
and live nowhere near Colorado as I once did.
And I don't know how many more walks like this
we will have together, these our most ordinary walks,
and I'm trying to hold this space as something sacred,
even with a dozen or more cigarette butts littering
the ground under my feet and a lasso of fish wire dangling
from a branch, and if the wire gets into the pond it will
likely strangle a great blue heron or some fish, which
are likely already done for (a signpost says, "This water
may have been contaminated with chemicals")—which
pisses me off—was it or wasn't it, and who is minding
this water anyway? Water that nevertheless looks serene
and beautiful under the setting sun. We start walking home

when I notice that the swan we'd seen earlier is now
gliding toward the swan on the far side. And I name
the one swan *acceptance* and the other swan *grief*.

## WHAT I DO AFTER MY HUSBAND'S LAST BREAKFAST AT HOME BEFORE MOVING TO MEMORY CARE

I walk upstairs to the bedroom, scrunch the collar of his plaid
L. L. Bean Nightwatch pajamas.
under my nose and inhale
his traces—spicy, slightly sweet.

Wash out the bits of food stuck in his three toothbrushes.

Listen to the hum of forced air through the register and watch my cat
sprawl across it for warmth.

I study the splotches of messy snow out the window that keep falling
and keep falling.

Reheat my coffee, sit down at the table, noticing how fast my heart
is racing.

I cry a little more.

I hear the snow begin to roar.

I spit up some mucus from the virus I've had for weeks.

Notice a nick near the quick of my left thumbnail, rub and rub my
index finger over it as if I can keep it from breaking.

HERE AT HOME

It's late now. You were beautiful.

I tumbled carelessly. How could I
have known any of this would become my life.

Sleeping and waking, days and years

still chime through. The you I took, most days, for granted.
Criticized. The you I turned to in bed each night.

Yesterday, you said, *I miss you.*

The hardest decibels of you. How long it's been
since I last touched your mind. Would be too hard

to show you the pots I've planted on the front porch

to cheer me, orange yellow lantana and purple liatris.
I can't keep you safe. And I never say, when you ask

where I'm going, *home.*

The evening will pass. You're alive
but you will never live here again.

I'll try to make the groundlessness feel like nothing

I need to make into a sad story. Here at home
the walls refuse to speak. But tonight—

maybe because I'm talking to you with my pen—

UNDER THE OVERPASS OFF THE 405 NORTH

After I'd claimed my suitcase from the rumble
of the rotating carousel at LAX, after I'd caught
the Flyaway bus and we'd barreled into the smog
and wall-to-wall on the 405 North, after the exit ramp
curving down and around it, for just a second
I saw them, they were like three farmers tilling a field,
two men from the highway maintenance crew
in orange reflective vests cropping a patch of grass
with rotating trimmers and a third man paring the slope—
you couldn't call it a garden, it was sparse and not
particularly beautiful, a few trees, a bird or two
probably chirping as we drove by—but it was as if
the part of me that had shut down and grown numb
had swallowed a shot of ginger with turmeric—
in less time than it takes to write *less time,* I was
revived by this nearly eye-to-eye respite from greed
and speed and need—and sure, this was just a job
and likely doesn't pay well, and I bet those vests
are itchy in the heat, these men eager for their break
or the end of their shift, but they were trimming
the weeds with whirling blades that seemed as tender
as a barber's shaver shearing the nape of a man's neck,
and I'm preserving this scene as if it were hoshagaki,
those Japanese dried persimmons which I just misspelled
as *permission,* I'm letting the sugar crystallize and bloom
into the orange vests the three men were wearing,
I'm letting myself pasture in a patch of earth, a little
tended, a little mended, in the bend of a highway.

## LET HEALING COME

*—after Jane Kenyon*

Let healing come
in ordinary time to the tattered
boughs of the fir tree cloaked in snow.

Let it come to my sadness
walking past Santa and Rudolf sprawled
flat on their backs on a dew-glistened lawn.

To the family of wild turkeys in the swale
behind Oak Street scavenging
birdseed chaff from my feeder.

Let it come to the boy in the Domino's van
delivering a small cheese pizza to the man
down the block who shelters alone.

To the stricken in sealed-off rooms, in silence,
in vanishing, and to their loved ones,
who dip their hands in grief.

Let it come to the trucker driving
his fourteen-wheeler all night
down I-95, hauling lumber.

To the blue heron on the bank
of Willow Pond tuning her wings
to the key of wind.

To the green snake, to the ant,
to the sweetgum tree
that knows trembling.

And to the sorry, to the hardened,
to the amber shard of sea-glass, to the moon
that burnishes the sea's brokenness,

and to you, beloved, may you wake
to trillium and bloodroot, marsh marigold
and bluebells that spring wild and greening

from the hard swill of earth.
May you bend the day close.

## SUPERMOON

OK, I admit it, I was chasing it, and when I shouted
*Hurry up!* you tripped a little as you were inching down

the steep stairs from the driveway to our summer rental.
Darling, you could have fallen, could have died.

All because I saw that sumptuous supermoon rising,
nothing blue about it but the *oo* about it, huge

and orange as kerosene burning through the pines,
pouring buckets of lava over the lake, and I rushed

to unlock the front door, race through the living
room out to the deck to snap photo after photo.

And of course it was too dark by then and no photo
could have captured it—and why do I keep trying

to hold a moon far too large for my arms, when you
are right here to hold? My burning has often been

too bright for both of us—as if I could only melt into
the foil of that clueless moon, I could keep us both

from waning.

## Notes

The italicized words in brackets in the reconstructed Sapphic fragments and erasures are from *If Not, Winter: Fragments of Sappho*, translated by Anne Carson, Vintage Books, 2003.

"Notes from Bar Harbor": *the roses / Had the look of flowers that are looked at* is from T. S. Eliot, *The Four Quartets*.

EPILOGUE

This afternoon you asked,
when we were having tea at the bookstore,
*Where do you think Wendy is?*
I saw myself moving away
from myself the way this evening
the moon is rising higher, diminishing
through the pines. Maybe the trees will
enjoy lightening themselves
down to their bones. Maybe they're more
themselves that way. I may be most
myself when I am watching them.

# Acknowledgments

*Autumn Sky Poetry Daily:* "How to Make Even a Little of It Slow Down," "At Hanson's Farm"

*Bait/Switch:* "Harvest of What Remains"

*Cider Press Review:* "Bees Murmur in the Language of the Hive"

*Hanging Loose:* "Ode to the Man at the Flying Fish Restaurant"

*Hare's Paw:* "Oh, Bright Star"

*Ibbetson Street:* "On the Car Radio, Von Biber's Ciacona in D Major," "Whether a Forest Is Like Quicksand if You're Lost in It"

*Lily Poetry Review:* "Field of Rocking Horses," "Two Dead Dolphins, Blackfish Creek, Wellfleet," "Counting My Blessings"

*Mid-American Review:* "Notes from Bar Harbor"

*One Art:* "Walking the Woods with You on the Day of Atonement"

*Nixes Mate Review:* "Ode to My Husband's Underwear," "Erasure of Reconstructed Sapphic Fragment 19," "Reconstructed Sapphic Fragment 43"

*Pangyrus:* "Reconstructed Sapphic Fragment 145," "Erasure of Reconstructed Fragment 145"

*Pencil Magazine, Issue Two, the Eraser Issue:* "Reconstructed Sapphic Fragment 83," "Erasure of Reconstructed Fragment 83"

*Pensive: A Global Journal of Spirituality & the Arts:* "Let Healing Come"

*South Florida Poetry Review:* "Love Is a Wishbone Caught in My Throat," "Jamie Wyeth Crushed a Strand of His Wife's Pearls," "Reversing Your Diagnosis," "Haibun," "Sitting with My Husband on a Bench in Front of Clay Pond"

*spoKe 10:* "I Ask My Husband's Neurologist About Alzheimer's and the Uncanny Valley" and "My Husband's Neurologist Answers My Questions About Alzheimer's and the Uncanny Valley" (appeared as one poem) and "Clover Food Lab"

*The Hudson Review:* "Reconstructed Sapphic Fragment 24C"

*The Red Letters, a Community of Voices,* edited by Steve Ratiner: "In the Kitchen" and "Under the Overpass on the 405 North"

*Thin Places & Sacred Spaces,* an anthology published by the *Amethyst Review:* "Mark Rothko, 'Untitled,' 1954"

*Twelve Mile Review:* "No Winter" and "Reconstructed Sapphic Fragment 67B"

"Alzheimer's Abecedarian" was a finalist for the Samuel Washington Allen Prize from the New England Poetry Club, 2025.

"Letters to the Beloved Written on Eggshells" was a collaboration with visual artist Connie Saems and was exhibited at Gallery Twist, Lexington, Massachusetts, May 17–June 9, 2024.

"Gossip and Metaphysics" was a finalist for the Amy Lowell Prize from the New England Poetry Club, 2024.

"The Way These Opalescent Balls Glow" won honorable mention from Art on the Trails *Number 9* at the Elaine and Phillip Beals Preserve, 2025.

※ ※ ※

I offer a deep bow to the many friends, colleagues, caregivers, and medical providers who have been essential to this book and this journey. To my poet kin who have supported me with their friendship, generosity, and crucial feedback on nearly all the poems in this book: Cynthia Bargar, Vivian Eyre, Xialoy Li, Steve Nickman, Verandah Porche, Sarah Dickenson Snyder, Connemara Wadsworth, and Margot Wizansky. With special thanks to Vivian Eyre for inviting me to your home where the poems in this book first came together, and for your valuable insights on organizing my manuscript.

To Christine Jones, my wonderful editor at Lily Poetry Review Books, for lending your counsel as the manuscript came together and for offering me detailed and creative feedback; and to Lily Editor in Chief Eileen Cleary—with gratitude for giving my book a beautiful and loving home and with admiration for all you do. To my friend Dalia Geffen, for catching and polishing all the scratches.

To my friend and visual collaborator Connie Saems, for your amazing drawings in this book, which beautifully enrich and intertwine with the text, allowing ineffable flickers and depths of meaning to emerge; and for the great gift of your creativity.

To Dr. Alvaro Pascual-Leone, my husband's sterling neurologist at the Wolk Center for Memory Health; and to esteemed poet friends and colleagues Lloyd Schwartz and Sarah Dickenson Snyder, for your generosity in taking the time to read my manuscript and for your kind words gracing the back of this book.

To Rachel Zucker and all those in my Reading with Rachel and Real People community for stimulating conversations around issues of writing about people in our lives.

To all the caregivers who have provided loving and generous care for my husband: you have gone above and beyond. Without question I would not have made it through the last few years without your support, especially that of Leide Crossley. We are so blessed to have you in our lives. With thanks for the kindness of Marta Fagundes. To the staff and caregivers at Bridges by Epoch at Lexington, especially Luidja, Shea, Camille, and Parkeuse, for your responsiveness and care. To my geriatric care manager Tammy Pozerycki, with gratitude for your insights, compassion, and problem solving. Much appreciation to the caregivers in the Rogerson House Adult Day Program, especially Ellie; and to Seniors Helping Seniors, with thanks for the caregiving companions you provided in the early days.

To the team of medical providers who have helped me keep my sanity, informed my understanding of Alzheimer's, and whose counsel has eased the brutality of its course, my deep appreciation, especially the team at the Wolk Center for Memory Health for your interdisciplinary approach to supporting the whole family, and to Medical Director Dr. Alvaro Pascual-Leone, who has been generous with his time and wise with his suggestions for maintaining cognitive reserve. And to psychologist Dr. Maggie Syme—I'm so grateful for your deep listening, steady understanding, and wise counsel.

I would not have been able to complete this book or this journey without the love, support, and direct care of my children. To Julia and Noah, you add such happiness, love, and faith to my life. And to Hannah and Kayden, so much joy. To Josh, Victor, and Andrew, who've helped in multiple ways in supporting me and your father. And to Nora for your clear head and compassionate heart.

To my many friends who have been there when the going has been rough: you know who you are. Thank you for sharing joys and sorrows.

And to my loving husband Herb—I'm so grateful for our twenty-six years together, and for your love, values, intellect, and kindness. While I fervently wish you had never developed Alzheimer's, the other side of having to endure it has been my ever-deepening compassion— in that, you have been my teacher.

# BEES MURMUR IN THE LANGUAGE OF THE HIVE

*—for my poetry sisters*

Oh, my blood sisters. Ask me,
I'll bathe and jelly the queen.
Baby the grubs as my own.

Lonely no more. And work to be done:
filling myself with nectar, lining
the shelves with wax
like any stockgirl.

I'll scout and scurry. I'll stamp
my bare feet and waggle my belly
to spell for you the *where*
of the marigolds, the *there* of the thyme,
the *now* of the peony.

I'm strumming my wings
like a harp to show you how far to fly,
embroidering my amazement
to bee balm, to hedge, and to sage.

Our bodies a roar. A duty.

## About Wendy Drexler

*Photo by Debi Milligan*

Wendy Drexler is a recipient of a 2022 artist fellowship from the Massachusetts Cultural Council. She is the author of three previous collections: *Western Motel* (Turning Point, 2012), *Before There Was Before* (Iris Press, 2017), and *Notes from the Column of Memory* (Terrapin, 2022). Her poems have appeared in *Barrow Street, J Journal, Mid-American Review, Nimrod, Pangyrus, Prairie Schooner, The Sun,* and *The Threepenny Review,* among others. She was awarded the 2025 E.E. Cummings prize from the New England Poetry Club. A recipient of the Juror's Prize for Art on the Trails, Southborough, MA, in 2021, Wendy served as poet in residence at New Mission High School in Hyde Park, MA, from 2018–2023, and as programming co-chair for the New England Poetry Club from 2016–2024. She currently serves on the Club's advisory board.

wendydrexlerpoetry.com

## About Connie Saems

Connie Saems is a visual artist based in Cambridge and Wellfleet, Massachusetts. Her work utilizes the power of language to augment form, transforming letters from poems into continuous lines that reflect her personal responses to the text. Deeply influenced by an interest in communication across cultures, her practice explores how language functions visually as both meaning and structure.

Connie's art has recently appeared in *Woven Tales Press* (Fall 2025), *Pencil Magazine* (Issue Two, Fall 2025), and *Limb of Water* by Christine Bess Jones (Fall 2025). She received a BFA from the University of the Arts in Philadelphia and has exhibited widely throughout Massachusetts. She has taught at institutions including Harvard University Office for the Arts, the Boston Center for Adult Education, and ARTSCAPE Cape Cod, and previously served as a docent at the Institute of Contemporary Art, Boston.

Saems.connie@comcast.net
www.conniesaems.com

www.ingramcontent.com/pod-product-compliance
Lightning Source LLC
Chambersburg PA
CBHW020407130626
46549CB00006B/2474